A declaration of love

The method of salvation through Jesus Christ

Samuel Davies

EVANGELICAL PRESS

EVANGELICAL PRESS
Grange Close, Faverdale North Industrial Estate, Darlington, Co. Durham, DL3 0PH, England

© Evangelical Press 1998. All rights reserved. No part of this publication may be reproduced, stored in a retrieval system or transmitted, in any form, or by any means, electronic, mechanical, photocopying, recording or otherwise, without the prior permission of the publishers.

Original sermon previously published in the USA.
This edition first published 1998

British Library Cataloguing in Publication Data available

ISBN 0 85234 408 2

Printed and bound in Great Britain by Bailes, Houghton-le-Spring, Tyne & Wear

Preface

Samuel Davies was born in the state of Delaware on 3 November 1723. His father, a farmer of Welsh extraction, was well known and respected for the quality of his Christian life and witness. His mother, also of Welsh origins, was known both for her intellectual ability and for her deep piety and devotion to the Lord. Young Samuel, like his biblical namesake, was born in answer to his mother's prayers and was solemnly consecrated to the Lord and his service from his childhood. In the absence of any suitable school in the neighbourhood it was his mother who was responsible for Samuel's early education and her godly instruction and example had a profound influence on him in his formative years.

The exact date and circumstances of Davies' conversion are not known. He made a public profession of faith in Christ at the age of fifteen, but there is evidence of a work of God's grace in his life by the time he was twelve years of age, or possibly even earlier. He devoted his whole energies to his studies in preparation for the Christian ministry and after a short period of instruction from a Baptist minister he completed his theological training at the school founded by Rev. Samuel Blair at Foggs Manor in Pennsylvania.

He was formally licensed to preach in July 1746 and ordained as an evangelist the following year with a special mission to serve a group of Dissenting congregations in Virginia. This particular appointment was a very sensitive one in the political and legal situation prevailing at the time and Davies' selection for it at this early stage in his ministry marks him out as a man of great delicacy and tact as well as a powerful preacher who combined a considerable degree of eloquence with the ability to present the truth of God in a clear, direct and simple way. His initial appointment was for a period of four months but his ministry was so well received that a call was soon issued to him to settle permanently in Virginia. By 1748 he was responsible for preaching at seven widely scattered meeting-places and also frequently travelled to other, largely unevangelized, areas to preach the gospel.

Such a busy schedule would have taxed the energies of the strongest man, but Samuel Davies was far from well. He had suffered from poor health, and in particular a tendency to hectic fevers, since his student days and his condition deteriorated following the shock caused by the death of his wife Sarah, whom he had married in October 1746, shortly after the completion of his initial four-month appointment to Virginia. However, the consciousness that he might only have a short time to live merely gave him a heightened sense of urgency to carry out his responsibilities as a preacher to the best of his ability in the time remaining to him.

The spring of 1748 saw a marked improvement in his health and in October of that year he married his second wife, Jane, a fine Christian lady who was to be a great support to him in his subsequent ministry and was to become the mother of his six children.

In 1753 Davies accompanied Gilbert Tennent, the celebrated preacher of the Great Awakening and founder of

A declaration of love

the Log College, to Britain on a preaching tour designed to awaken interest in, and raise funds for, the work of the gospel in Virginia, and in particular for the founding of the College of New Jersey, later to be renamed Princeton College. The tour was not only a great success but gave Davies the opportunity to make the acquaintance of many of the notable Dissenting ministers in England at that time.

In 1758, following the death of Jonathan Edwards, Davies was chosen to succeed him as president of the college, the founding of which he had been so active in promoting. At first he was reluctant to accept, or to leave his pastoral responsibilities in Virginia for Princeton, but he finally took up the appointment in July 1759 and was formally inaugurated as president of the college in September of that year. He brought to this position the same enthusiasm, commitment and level of exertion that he had manifested in his labours as a pastor and evangelist and under his leadership the college rose to new heights of usefulness in the Lord's service. Sadly, his tenure of this office was destined to be short, for in February 1761 he contracted pneumonia, which led to a brain fever and from which he died, at the age of only thirty-seven.

Samuel Davies' ministry coincided with the period of widespread and remarkable revival which has come to be known in history as the Great Awakening. That he should on more than one occasion in his relatively short ministry be singled out as the man most fitted to perform a task or occupy a position of especial responsibility — not least at a time when so many preachers were being used in a remarkable way — is an eloquent testimony to the quality of his character and his gifts as preacher and pastor.

Samuel Davies is remembered for his oratory, his academic leadership as college president, his championship of the rights to freedom to worship of Dissenting congregations, his support for pioneer missionary work among the North American Indians and especially for his loving pastoral concern for the spiritual welfare of all those among whom he ministered. But first and foremost he was a preacher of God's Word and one of the most highly regarded evangelists of his day. It is hoped that in presenting one of his sermons in a new version for the modern reader, this preacher of former times may once again speak powerfully to the hearts of men and women today.

Editing of the text has been limited to a minimum. A few archaic sentence structures and expressions have been omitted or replaced with more modern equivalents. While the author's original headings have been retained in the body of the text, a number of additional headings have been inserted to make the flow of his thought more immediately obvious to the reader. Some passages, in which he directly addresses his congregation, have also been amended to reflect the fact that the message is now being presented in a written form rather than preached to an assembled congregation. Throughout the aim has been to make the preaching of Davies more accessible to the modern reader while retaining its original character. All Scripture quotations have been taken from the Authorized/King James Version, as in the original sermon.

A declaration of love

The method of salvation through Jesus Christ

'For God so loved the world, that he gave his only begotten Son, that whosoever believeth in him should not perish, but have everlasting life' (John 3:16).

I have been giving much serious thought to the question in what way my life, redeemed from the grave,[1] may be of most service to you, my dear readers, and I would collect all my feeble remaining strength into one vigorous effort in order to bring you the greatest possible benefit. If I knew what subject was the most fitted to bring about the salvation of your souls, that is the subject to which my heart would cling with special fondness, and which I would make the matter of the present message.

I am particularly conscious that I am addressing those who by nature are sinners — guilty, depraved, helpless creatures — and that, if you are ever to be saved, it will be only through Jesus Christ, in the way that the gospel reveals. I know that your everlasting life and happiness hinge on the reception you give to this Saviour and this way of salvation. When I consider these things, I can think of no subject I can more properly choose than to set forth the Lord Jesus as the Saviour whom you need, and to explain and impress on you the method of salvation through his mediation; or, in other words, to preach the pure gospel to you; for the gospel, in the most proper sense, is nothing else but a revelation of a way of salvation for sinners of Adam's race.

My text furnishes me with suitable materials for my purpose. Let heaven and earth hear it with wonder, joy and raptures of praise! 'God so loved the world, that he gave his only begotten Son, that whosoever [or that everyone that] believeth in him should not perish, but have everlasting life.'

This is a part of the most important evening conversation that ever was held — I mean the conversation between Christ and Nicodemus, a Pharisee and ruler of the Jews. Our Lord first instructs him in the doctrine of regeneration, that great and essential element of what constitutes a Christian and prerequisite to our admission to the kingdom of heaven. Then he proceeds to inform him of the gospel method of salvation, which contains these two essential truths: the death of Christ, as the great foundation of blessedness; and faith in him, as the great qualification on the sinner's part.

He presents this important doctrine to us in various forms, with a very significant repetition: 'As Moses lifted up the serpent in the wilderness, even so must the Son of Man be lifted up', that is, hung high on a cross, 'that whosoever believeth in him should not perish, but have eternal life.' Then follows my text, which expresses the same doctrine with great force: 'God so loved the world, that he gave his only begotten Son [gave him up to death], that whosoever believeth in him should not perish, but have everlasting life' (John 3:14-16).

He goes on to mention something truly wonderful. This earth is a rebellious province of Jehovah's dominions, and therefore if his Son should ever visit it, one would think it would be as an angry judge, or as the executioner of his Father's vengeance. But, astonishing as it is, 'God sent not his Son into the world to condemn the world; but that the world through him might be saved.' Hence the terms of life and death are fixed: 'He that believeth on him is not condemned: but he that believeth not is condemned already, because he hath not believed in the name of the only begotten Son of God' (John 3:17,18). What heavenly rivers of pleasure flow in these verses! Never, surely, was there so much gospel expressed in so few words. Here you may see the whole of the gospel in miniature and bind it to your hearts for ever. These verses alone, it seems to me, are a sufficient remedy for a dying world.

The truths I would infer from the text for our present consideration are these: that without Christ all who read these words are in a perishing condition; that through Jesus Christ a way is opened for your salvation; that the essential prerequisite to your being saved in this way is faith in Jesus Christ; that everyone, without exception, whatever his former character may have been, that is enabled to comply with this prerequisite will certainly be saved; and that the way in which this salvation is accomplished, or the mission of Christ into our world as the Saviour of sinners, is a most striking and astonishing instance and display of the love of God.

1. Without Christ you are in a perishing condition

My text implies that without Christ you, my dear readers, are in a perishing condition. This holds true of you in particular because it holds true of the world universally, for the world was undoubtedly in a perishing condition without Christ, and none but he could rescue it; otherwise God would never have given his only begotten Son to save it. God is not ostentatious or prodigal with his gifts, especially not such an inestimable gift as his Son, whom he loves infinitely more than the whole of creation. So great, so dear a person would not have been sent upon a mission which could have been discharged by any other being. Thousands of rams must rather have bled in sacrifice, or ten thousands of rivers of oil have flowed; our first-born must have been made to die for our transgressions, the fruit of our bodies for the sin of our souls; Gabriel or some of the upper ranks of angels must rather have left their thrones and hung on a cross, if any such methods of salvation had been sufficient. All this would have been nothing in comparison with what is involved in the only begotten Son of God leaving his native heaven and all its glories, assuming our degraded nature, spending thirty-three long and tedious years in poverty, disgrace and persecution, dying as a criminal and a slave in the midst of ignominy and torture and lying in a grave as a mangled, breathless corpse. We may be sure there was the highest degree of necessity for it; otherwise God would not have given up his dear Son to such horrid sufferings.

This, then, was the true state of the world, and consequently yours without Christ: it was hopeless and desperate, however it is viewed. The state of the world was so bad that men would not even have tried the efficacy of sacrifices, prayers, tears, reformation and repentance — or if they had tried them, it would have been in vain. It would have been inconsistent with maintaining the honour of the perfections of God's character or of his righteous government to admit sacrifices, prayers, tears, repentance and reformation as a sufficient atonement.

What a melancholy view of the world we now have before us! We know the state of mankind only under the gracious government of a Mediator, and we very seldom realize what our miserable condition would have been, had this gracious method of salvation never been set up. But imagine for a moment a world without a Saviour, and then take a view of it: helpless, hopeless, under the righteous displeasure of God and despairing of relief! It would have been the very suburbs of hell, the haunt of devils, a place where guilt, misery and despair reign, the mouth of the infernal pit, the gate of hell itself! This would have been the condition of our world had it not been for Jesus, who redeemed it, and yet in this very world he is neglected and despised.

Why is the world in such a hopeless condition?

But you may ask, 'How does it come about that the world was in such an undone, helpless and hopeless condition without Christ?' or 'What are the reasons for all this?'

The true account of this will appear from these two considerations: that all mankind are sinners and that by no other method than the mediation of Christ can the salvation of sinners be made consistent with upholding the perfections of God's character and the honour of his government, with the public good, or even with the very nature of things.

All mankind are sinners

This is too evident to need proof. They are sinners, rebels against the greatest and best of beings, against their Maker, their liberal Benefactor and their rightful Sovereign, to whom they are under greater and more pressing obligations than they can be to any creature, or even to the entire system of creatures. All, in every part of our guilty globe, are sinners and rebels. There is none righteous — no, not one. All, without exception, are sinners — from age to age for thousands of years. There have been thousands, millions, innumerable multitudes of sinners.

What an obnoxious race this is! There appears to be no difficulty that would stand in the way of justice to prevent the punishment of such creatures. But what seemingly insuperable difficulties appear to stand in the way of their salvation! Let me mention a few of them to help you to appreciate how blessed is the Saviour who has removed them all.

Obstacles in the way of the salvation of sinners

If such sinners are to be saved, how are *the holiness and justice of God* to be displayed? How is he to present to all the universe an honourable view of himself as a being of perfect purity and one who is an enemy to all moral evil?

If such sinners are to be saved, how shall *the honour of the divine government and law* be upheld? How will the dignity of the law appear, if a race of rebels may trifle with it with impunity? What a sorry law it must be if there are no sanctions to enforce it, or if such sanctions may be dispensed with at will! What a contemptible government — that may be insulted and rejected, and the offender restored to favour without punishment or without being made an example to others! No government can survive on such principles of excessive indulgence.

How can such sinners be saved, and yet *the good of the public* be secured — which is always the objective of every wise and good ruler? By the public good I do not mean the happiness of mankind alone, but the happiness of the whole created universe taken collectively — in comparison with which the happiness of men may be only a private interest (and private interests should always give way to the public good).

Now sin has a direct tendency, according to the nature of things, to scatter misery and ruin wherever its infection reaches. Therefore the public good requires that a loud and effectual warning should be given against all sin and that offenders should be dealt with in such a manner as to deter others from offending. But how can this be done? How can the sinner be saved, and yet the evil of sin be displayed and all other beings deterred from committing it for ever? How can sin be discouraged by pardoning it? How can its evil be displayed by letting the criminal escape punishment? These are such difficulties that nothing but divine wisdom could ever surmount them.

These difficulties lie in the way of a mere pardon and exemption from punishment, but salvation includes more than this. When sinners are saved, they are not only pardoned, but received into high favour, made the children, the friends, the courtiers of the King of heaven. They are not only delivered from punishment, but also raised to the enjoyment of a state of perfect positive happiness, and nothing short of this can truly make creatures like us happy. Now, looked at in this light, the difficulties rise still higher.

This point is all the more worthy of our observation since it is not generally the case in matters relating to human government; and as men are apt to form their notions of the divine government by human examples, they are less conscious of these difficulties. But this is indeed the true state of the case here: how can the sinner be not only delivered from punishment but also raised to a state of perfect happiness? How can he not only escape the displeasure of his offended Sovereign, but be received into full favour and elevated to a position of the highest honour and dignity?

How can all this be done without casting a cloud over the purity and justice of the Lord of all, without sinking his law and government into contempt, without diminishing the evil of sin and emboldening others to dare to engage in it themselves — and so at once injuring both the character of the supreme Ruler and the public good? How can sinners, I repeat, be saved without their salvation entailing these bad consequences?

God must act in his character of supreme Judge

Now here it is important to remember that provision must be made against these consequences. To save men at random without considering the consequences, to distribute happiness to individuals with a hand that failed to make any distinction between them — this would be at once inconsistent with the character of the supreme Magistrate of the universe and with the public good.

Persons acting in a private capacity are at liberty to forgive private offences — indeed, it is their duty to forgive — and they can hardly offend by way of excess in the generous virtues of mercy and compassion. But it is not the same for a magistrate: he is obliged to act in accordance with the dignity of his government and the interests of the public, and he may therefore easily carry his leniency to a very dangerous extreme and by his tenderness to criminals do an extensive injury to the state.

A declaration of love

This is particularly the case with regard to the great God, the universal Magistrate of all creation. And this ought to be seriously considered by those men of loose principles among us who look upon God only under the fond character of a Father, or a being of infinite mercy, and therefore conclude that they have little to fear from him in spite of all their flagrant violations of his laws. There is no absolute necessity that sinners should be saved; justice may be allowed to take its course where they are concerned. But there is the most absolute necessity that the Ruler of the world should both be, and appear to be, holy and just. There is the most absolute necessity that he should support the dignity of his government and guard it from contempt, that he should strike all creation with a proper horror of sin and represent it in its genuine infernal colours, and so act in the interests of the good of the whole, rather than a part.

There is, I say, the highest and most absolute necessity for these things; and they cannot be dispensed with as if they were the result of some arbitrary decision which may be rescinded at will. And unless these objectives can be met in the salvation of men, men cannot be saved at all. No, they must all perish, rather than that God should act out of character, as the supreme Magistrate of the universe, or bestow private favours on criminals, to the detriment of the public well-being.

An apparently insuperable difficulty

And in this lay the difficulty. Call a council of all the sages and wise men of the world, and they can never get over this difficulty without borrowing assistance from the gospel. Indeed, this no doubt puzzled the intelligence of all the angels who pry so deep into the mysteries of heaven, before the gospel was fully revealed. I feel sure that the angels, when they saw the fall of men, gave him up as a desperate case. 'Alas!' they cried. 'The poor creature is gone! He and all his numerous race are lost for ever.' This, they knew, had been the doom of their fellow-angels that sinned, and could they hope anything better for man? They had not then seen any of the wonders of pardoning love and mercy, and could they have once thought that the glorious person who occupied the middle throne and was their Creator and Lord would ever become a man and die like a criminal to redeem creatures of an inferior rank? No, they would probably have shuddered at such a thought as blasphemy.

And must we, then, give up ourselves and all our race as lost beyond recovery? There are huge and seemingly insuperable difficulties in the way and we have seen that neither men nor angels can prescribe any solution. But, 'Sing, O ye heavens; for the Lord hath done it: shout, ye lower parts of the earth: break forth into singing, ye mountains, O forest, and every tree therein: for the Lord hath redeemed Jacob, and glorified himself in Israel' (Isa. 44:23). Which leads me to my next point.

2. Through Jesus Christ a way is opened up for salvation

My text implies, secondly, that through Jesus Christ a way is opened up for your salvation. He, and only he, was found equal to the undertaking, and before him all these mountains became a plain; all these difficulties vanished. Now God can be just, can secure the dignity of his character as the Ruler of the world and meet all the objectives of government, and yet justify and save the sinner who believes in Jesus.

This is plainly implied in this glorious summary of the gospel: 'God so loved the world, that he gave his only begotten Son, that whosoever believeth in him should not perish, but have everlasting life.' Without this gift all was lost, but now whoever believes in him may be saved, and saved in a most honourable way. This will be seen more clearly if we consider the ways in which the mediation of Christ was fitted to remove the difficulties mentioned. But I would begin by making two general remarks.

The punishment must fulfil the purposes of government

The first is that God must be considered in this affair as acting in his public character, as Supreme Magistrate, or Governor, of the world. Therefore all the punishment which he is concerned to see inflicted upon sin is only such as fulfils the purposes of government. Private revenge must vent itself on the very person of the offender, or be disappointed. But to a ruler, acting in his official capacity, it may in some cases be a matter of indifference whether the punishment is sustained by the very person who offended, or by a substitute suffering in his place. It may also be a matter of indifference whether the very same punishment that is laid down in the law, as to kind and degree, or a punishment equivalent to it is to be inflicted. Provided that the honour of the ruler and his government are maintained, that he can be seen not to countenance any form of disobedience — if, in short, all the objectives of government can be met — such things as these are matters of indifference. Consequently, if these ends were to be met by Christ's suffering in the place of sinners, there would be no objection against it.

The person of Christ fits him to meet these requirements

This remark introduces another — namely that, because of who Jesus Christ is, his suffering as the substitute, or surety, of sinners fulfils all the requirements of government which could be satisfied by punishing the sinners themselves. To impose suffering upon the innocent, when they are unwilling, is unjust, but Jesus was willing to undertake the dreadful task. And besides, he was a person at his own disposal — his own property, so to speak — and therefore he had a right to dispose of his life as he pleased. There was, therefore, a merit in his agreeing to something that he was not obliged to undertake had he not consented to do so. He was also a person of infinite dignity, and infinitely beloved by his Father. All these considerations combined to render the merit of his sufferings, though only endured for a short time and of a different kind of punishment from that of hell, equal — indeed, more than equal — to the everlasting sufferings of sinners themselves.

Jesus Christ was also above law — that is, not obliged to be subject to the law which he had made for his creatures. Consequently his obedience to the law, not being necessary on his own account, might be imputed to others. Mere creatures, on the other hand, are incapable of works of supererogation — that is, of doing more than they are bound to do — since they are obliged to obey their divine Lawgiver on their own account, to the utmost extent of their abilities. Consequently, their obedience, however perfect, can be sufficient only for themselves, and cannot be imputed to others.

Thus it appears, in general, that the requirements of government are as effectually met by the sufferings of Christ in the place of sinners as they could be by the everlasting

A declaration of love

punishment of the sinners themselves; indeed, as we proceed, we shall find they are met in a more striking and illustrious manner.

The death of Christ reveals God's holiness and justice

To mention particulars, first, was it necessary that the holiness and justice of God should be displayed in the salvation of sinners? See how brightly they shine in a suffering Saviour! Now it appears that such is the holiness and justice of God that he will not let even his own Son escape unpunished, when he stands, in the eyes of the law, in the place of sinners, even though he was guilty only by the slight stain (if I may put it this way) of imputation. Could the execution of everlasting punishment upon the hateful criminals themselves ever give so bright a display of these attributes? It is impossible that it should.

The death of Christ upholds the honour of God's law

Again, was there a difficulty in finding a way of saving sinners, and yet at the same time maintaining the rights of the divine government and the honour of the law? See how this difficulty is removed by the obedience and death of Christ! Now it appears that the rights of the divine government are so sacred and inviolable that they must be maintained, even though the beloved Son of God should himself fall a sacrifice to justice, and that not one offence against this government can be pardoned without his making a full atonement. Now it appears that the Supreme Ruler is not to be trifled with, but that the injury done to his honour must be put right, even though it has to be at the expense of his Son's blood and life. Through Christ the precepts of the law are perfectly obeyed in every part and a full equivalent to the penalty it demands is endured by a person of infinite dignity. It is only on this footing — that is, of complete satisfaction to all the demands of the law — that any of the rebellious sons of men can be restored to favour.

This is a satisfaction which Christ alone could give; it is utterly impossible for sinners to give such satisfaction, either by doing or suffering. They cannot do all the things that are written in the law; nor can they endure the penalty it demands, without enduring eternal misery, and therefore the law has received a more complete satisfaction in Christ than it would ever receive from the offenders themselves.

The cross of Christ reveals sin for what it is

Or again, was there a difficulty in finding a way of saving sinners, while at the same time ensuring that the evil of sin is displayed in all its horrors? Go to the cross of Christ. There, you fools, who make a mock of sin, there you will learn how evil a thing sin is, and how hateful it is to the great God. There you may see that it is so great an evil that when it is merely imputed to the man that is God's fellow, in his role as the surety of sinners, it cannot escape punishment. No, when that dreadful stain lay upon him, immediately the commission was given to divine justice: 'Awake, O sword, against my Shepherd, and against the man that is my fellow, saith the Lord of hosts: smite the Shepherd' (Zech. 13:7). When Christ stood in the place of sinners even the Father did not spare his own Son, but gave him up to death. It would not be considered strange that the criminals themselves, who are an inferior race of creatures, should not escape punishment, but how great an evil sin must be if it cannot be overlooked even when the person charged with it is the favourite of heaven himself, the only begotten Son of God! Surely nothing else could give so striking a display of the evil nature of sin!

The cross of Christ is in the interests of the public good

Was there a difficulty in finding a way to reconcile the salvation of sinners with acting in the interests of the public good — that is, how to forgive sins and yet give an effectual warning against sin? Was there a problem over finding a way to receive the sinner into favour and raise him to the enjoyment of the highest honour and happiness, and yet at the same time to deter all other beings from offending? All this is provided for in the sufferings of Christ as a surety. Let all of creation look to his cross and receive the warning which his wounds, groans, blood and dying agonies proclaim aloud — and surely they can never dare to follow man's example in offending against God. Now they may see that the only instance of pardon to be found in the universe was brought about by such means as are not likely to be repeated — by the incarnation and death of the Lord of glory. Can they flatter themselves that he will leave his throne and hang upon a cross as often as any of his creatures may take it upon themselves to dare offend him? No. Such a miracle as this, the utmost effort of divine grace, is not something to be often repeated and, therefore, if they dare to sin, they do so at their peril. They have no reason to flatter themselves that they will be favoured like fallen man, but rather to expect that they will share in the doom of the fallen angels.

Or, if they were to think that sin may escape with only a slight punishment, here they may be convinced of the contrary. If the beloved of heaven, the Lord of glory, though personally innocent, suffers so much when sin is merely *imputed* to him, what shall the sinners themselves feel, who can claim no favour upon the footing of their own importance, or their personal innocence? If these things are done in the green tree, what shall be done in the dry?

The cross invites our wonder and praise

So, my brethren, you may see how a way is opened through Jesus Christ for our salvation. All the objectives of government are met and yet you may be pardoned and made happy. Those attributes of the divine nature, such as mercy and justice, which seemed to clash, are now reconciled; now their bright beams mingle and both shine with a brighter glory in the salvation of sinners than either of them could apart. And what about you? Are you not compelled to acknowledge this divine, Godlike scheme? Can you look around you over the works of the creation, and see the divine wisdom in every object, and yet not perceive the divine agency in this still more glorious work of redemption? To quote Young, redemption gives a full view of the Deity, not as the sun in eclipse, half dark, half bright, but as

>A God all o'er consummate, absolute,
>Full orb'd, in his whole round rays complete.

And shall not men and angels join in wonder and praise at the survey of this amazing scheme? Angels are rapt in wonder

A declaration of love

and praise, and will be so to all eternity. See how they pry into this mystery! Hark how they sing, 'Glory to God in the highest!' and celebrate the Lamb that was slain! And shall not men, who are personally interested in the affair, join with them? Oh! Are there none to join with them from among my readers? Surely none can refuse!

Now, since all obstacles are removed on God's part that lay in the way of our salvation, why should we not all be saved together? What is there to hinder our crowding into heaven indiscriminately? Or what is there required on our part, in order to make us partakers of this salvation? Here it is proper to pass on to the next truth inferred from the text.

3. The essential prerequisite to being saved is faith in Jesus Christ

The third point to be inferred from the text is that the one essential thing that is required if you are to be saved in this way is faith in Jesus Christ.

Why faith is essential

Though the obstacles on God's part are removed by the death of Christ, yet there is one still remaining in the sinner which cannot be removed without his consent and which, while it remains, renders his salvation impossible in the very nature of things — that is, the depravity and corruption of his nature. Till this is cured, he has no taste for those enjoyments and occupations in which the happiness of heaven consists, and consequently he cannot be happy there. Therefore there is a necessity, in the very nature of things, that he should be made holy, in order to be saved — indeed, his salvation itself consists in holiness. Now, faith is the root of all holiness in a sinner. Without a firm belief of the great truths of the gospel, based on a clear understanding of them, it is impossible that a sinner should be sanctified by the influence of those truths; and without a particular faith in Jesus Christ he cannot derive from Christ those sanctifying influences by which alone he can be made holy and which are conveyed to us through Jesus Christ, and through him alone.

Besides, it would be highly inappropriate, and indeed impossible, to save a sinner against his will, or in a way he dislikes. Now faith, as we shall see in a moment, principally consists in a hearty consent to, and approval of, the way of salvation through Jesus Christ — the only way in which a sinner can be saved that is consistent with the honour of God. So we see that the constitution of the gospel is not only just, but as merciful as it can be, when it ordains that only the one who believes shall be saved, but that the one who does not believe shall be damned.

Then again, we cannot be saved through Jesus Christ until his righteousness is so far made our own as to satisfy the requirements of the law on our behalf and procure for us the favour of God; but his righteousness cannot be imputed to us in this way, or accounted ours in law, till we are united to him in such a way as to be one person with him in the eyes of the law. Now faith is the bond that unites us to him; faith is that which gives us an interest in Christ. Therefore without faith we cannot receive any benefit from his righteousness.

A declaration of love

What is faith in Christ?

Here, then, a most interesting question arises: what is it to believe in Jesus Christ? Or, to put it another way, what is that faith which is the essential prerequisite to salvation? If you are capable of turning your thoughts to the most important question in the whole world, I urge you to give this matter your full attention, as befits so serious and solemn a subject.

Faith in Christ includes in it an element of speculation — that is, it includes a speculative but rational belief, based on the testimony of God, that Jesus Christ is the only Saviour of men. But yet it is not entirely speculative, like the faith of so many: it is a more practical, experimental thing. In order to understand its nature, you must take notice of the following particulars.

1. Faith presupposes a deep sense of our undone, helpless condition. I told you before that this is the condition of the world in general without Christ, and you must know in your heart that this is your condition in particular before you can believe in him as your Saviour. He came to be a Saviour in a desperate situation, when no deliverance could possibly be had from any other quarter, and you cannot receive him in that capacity till you feel yourself to be in such a situation. Therefore, in order for you to believe, all your pleas and excuses for your sins must be silenced; all your exalted views of your own goodness must be mortified; all your dependence upon your own righteousness — upon the merit of your prayers, your repentance and good works — must be done away with. You must feel that you are totally cast upon the mercy of God, that he may justly reject you for ever and that nothing that you can do can put him under any obligation to save you. You must be deeply conscious of these things; otherwise you can never receive the Lord Jesus Christ in that capacity in which he is set before you — namely, as a Saviour in a desperate situation.

I wish and pray that all who are reading this booklet may see themselves in this true, though mortifying light. It is for want of seeing things in this light that so many who hear the gospel remain unbelievers. It is for want of this that the Lord Jesus is so lightly esteemed, so little sought for, so little desired among us. In short, it is the failure to see themselves in this light that is the principal cause of so many perishing from under the very sound of the gospel and, as it were, from between the hands of a Saviour. It is this, alas! that causes them to perish, like the impenitent thief on the cross, with a Saviour by their side. Oh that you once rightly knew your own situation! You would then soon know Jesus Christ and receive salvation from his hand.

2. Faith implies the enlightening of the understanding to discover the suitability of Jesus Christ to be a Saviour, and the excellence of the way of salvation through him. While the sinner lies undone and helpless in himself, and looking about in vain for some deliverance, it pleases a gracious God to shine into his heart and enable him to see his glory in the face of Jesus Christ. Now this once-neglected Saviour appears not only absolutely necessary, but also all-glorious and lovely, and the sinner's heart is completely carried away and for ever captivated with his beauty. Now the neglected gospel appears in a new light — as different from all his former views of it as if it were quite another thing. Space

A declaration of love

does not permit me to expound at length upon this discovery of Christ and the gospel which comes with faith — and, indeed, should I dwell upon the subject at ever such great length, I still could not do justice to it in attempting to convey an idea of it to such of you as have never had the happiness of experiencing it for yourselves. In short, the Lord Jesus and the way of salvation through him appear perfectly suitable, all-sufficient and all-glorious.

3. In consequence of this, the sinner is enabled to embrace this Saviour with all his heart and to give a voluntary, cheerful consent to this glorious scheme of salvation. Now all his former unwillingness and reluctance are subdued, and his heart no longer draws back from the terms of the gospel, but he complies with them — and does so not merely out of constraint and necessity, but out of free choice, and with very great pleasure and delight. How his heart now clings to the dear Lord Jesus with the deepest affection and tenderness! He is lost in wonder, joy and gratitude at the view of the divine perfections as they are displayed in this method of redemption. He rejoices in it, as not only bringing happiness to him, but glory to God; as making his salvation not only consistent with, but a bright illustration of, the perfections of God's character and the dignity of his government. While he had only the low and selfish principles of corrupt human nature, he had no concern about the honour of God — if only he might be saved, that was all he was concerned about. But now he has a noble, generous heart; now he is concerned that God should be honoured in his salvation, and this method of salvation is made all the more precious to him by the thought that it secures to God the supremacy and makes his salvation subservient to the glory of God.

4. Faith in Jesus Christ implies a humble trust or dependence upon him alone for the pardon of sin, acceptance with God and every blessing. As I told you before, the sinner's self-confidence is mortified. He gives up all hopes of acceptance on the grounds of his own righteousness. He is filled with self-despair, and yet he does not altogether despair; he does not give up himself as lost, but has cheerful hopes of becoming a child of God and being for ever happy — guilty and unworthy as he is. And on what are these hopes founded? Why, on the mere free grace and mercy of God, through the righteousness of Jesus Christ. On this he ventures his guilty, unworthy, helpless soul, and finds it a firm, immovable foundation, while every other ground on which he might have depended proves a mere quicksand.

There are many who flatter themselves they put their trust in God, but their trust lacks various qualifications essential to a true faith. It is not the trust of a humble, helpless soul that draws all its encouragement from the mere mercy of God and the free indefinite offer of the gospel, but it is the presumptuous trust of a proud, self-confident sinner, who draws his encouragement, in part at least, from his own imaginary goodness and importance. It is not a trust in the mercy of God through Jesus Christ, as the only medium through whom that mercy can be honourably conveyed; but either in the mercy of God viewed in an absolute sense, without a proper reference to a Mediator, or in his mercy as being in some measure deserved, or moved, by something in the sinner. Examine whether your trust in God will stand this test.

The evidence of faith

I have now given you a brief answer to that great question:

A declaration of love

'What is it to believe in Jesus Christ?' and I hope you understand it, though I have not written about it at as great length as I should have liked to have done. I shall only add that this faith may also be known by the effects which it produces and which are inseparable from it. These are as follows. Faith purifies the heart and is a living principle of inward holiness. Faith is always productive of good works and leads us to universal obedience. Faith overcomes the world and all its temptations. Faith lays hold on the reality of eternal things and brings them near, and hence it is defined by the apostle as 'the substance of things hoped for, the evidence of things not seen' (Heb. 11:1).

Here I have a very important question to put to you: can you, dear reader, say, 'Well, in spite of all my imperfections and all my doubts and fears, I can only humbly hope, after the best examination I can make, that a faith has been produced in this heart of mine'? Can you indeed say so? Then I bring you glad tidings of great joy: you will be saved. Yes, saved is what you will be, in spite of earth and hell; you will be saved, however great your past sins have been. Which thought introduces the glorious truth that comes next in order.

4. Everyone who is enabled to believe in Christ will be saved

My text implies, next, that everyone, without exception, whatever his former character may have been, who is enabled to believe in Jesus Christ will certainly be saved. The number, or the serious nature, of the sins does not alter the case, and the reason for this is that the sinner is not received into favour, either in whole or in part, on account of anything personal, but solely and entirely on account of the righteousness of Jesus Christ. Now, this righteousness is perfectly equal to all the demands of the law and, therefore, when this righteousness is made over to the sinner as his by imputation, the law has no more demands upon him for great sins than for small, for many than for few; because all demands are fully satisfied by the obedience of Jesus Christ to the law. You see that sinners of all characters who believe in him are made equal in this respect: they are all admitted upon one common footing, the righteousness of Christ, and that is as sufficient for one as for another.

The promises of Scripture

This encouraging truth has the most abundant support from the Holy Scriptures. Observe that agreeably indefinite word 'whosoever' which is so often repeated: 'Whosoever believeth in him [shall] not perish, but have everlasting life.' Whoever he may be — however vile, however guilty, however unworthy — if he only believes, he shall not perish, but have everlasting life. What an agreeable assurance this is from the lips of the one who has the final destinies of men at his disposal! The same blessed lips have also declared, 'Him that cometh to me I will in no wise cast out' (John 6:37) and 'Whosoever will, let him take the water of life freely' (Rev. 22:17).

The men Christ chose when he was on earth

He has given you more than bare words to confirm you in the belief of this truth; this is also the principle upon which

A declaration of love

he has acted, choosing some of the most abandoned sinners to make them examples, not of his justice, as we might expect, but of his mercy, for the encouragement of others. In the days of his flesh he was reproached by his enemies for his friendship with 'publicans and sinners', but it is a sure fact that, instead of reproaching him on this account, we must love him for it.

When he rose from the dead, he did not rise with angry resentment against his murderers. No, instead he singles them out from a world of sinners, to make them the first offers of pardon through the blood which they had just shed. He orders 'that repentance and remission of sins should be preached in his name among all nations, beginning at Jerusalem' (Luke 24:47). At Jerusalem, where he had been crucified a few days before, there he orders the first proclamation of pardon and life to be made.

The example of the Corinthian church

You may see what great sinners he chose to make the monuments of his grace in Corinth: 'Neither fornicators, nor idolaters, nor adulterers, nor effeminate, nor abusers of themselves with mankind, nor thieves, nor covetous, nor drunkards, nor revilers, nor extortioners, shall inherit the kingdom of God.' What a dismal catalogue this is! It is no wonder that such a bunch of people should not inherit the kingdom of heaven! They are fit only for the punishment of hell and yet, astonishing as it is, the passage continues: 'Such were some of you: but ye are washed, but ye are sanctified, but ye are justified in the name of the Lord Jesus, and by the Spirit of our God' (1 Cor. 6:9-11). After this what sinner can despair of receiving mercy when he believes in Jesus?

The example of Paul

St Paul was another instance of the same kind: 'This,' says he, 'is a faithful saying [a saying that may be depended on as true], and worthy of all acceptation [from a guilty world], that Christ Jesus came into the world to save sinners; of whom I am chief. Howbeit for this cause I obtained mercy, that in me first Jesus Christ might show forth all long-suffering, for a pattern to them which should hereafter believe on him to life everlasting' (1 Tim. 1:15-16). A lesser sinner would not have served this purpose so well, but if Saul the persecutor obtains mercy when he believes, who can despair?

You see from all this, dear readers, that you are not excluded from Christ and from life by the fact that you are great sinners, so if you perish it must be from another cause: it must be on account of your wilful unbelief in not accepting Jesus Christ as your Saviour. If you reject him, then indeed you must perish, however small your sins have been; for it is only his death that can make atonement for even the slightest guilt, and if you have no personal interest in his death, the guilt of the smallest sin will sink you into ruin.

Here is a door wide enough for all who are reading these pages, if you will only enter in by faith. Come, then, enter in, those of you who up till now have been counted among the greatest of sinners, that have been ringleaders in evil — come now, take the lead, and show others the way to Jesus Christ! Though you may have been an immoral person, an embezzler, a thief or a murderer, there is salvation even for you, if you will only believe. Oh, how astonishing is the love of God discovered in this way! This consideration introduces the last inference to be made from my text.

5. The way in which this salvation is accomplished is a striking display of the love of God

Finally, my text implies that the means by which this salvation is accomplished, or the mission of the Saviour into our world, is a most striking and astonishing display of the love of God: 'God so loved the world, that he gave his only begotten Son...' View the scheme all through and you will discover love, infinite love, in every part of it.

Consider the great God as happy in himself and independent of all his creatures. What but love — self-motivated love — could move him to make such provision for one relatively insignificant section of his creation?

Consider the world sunk in sin, not only without merit, but most deserving of everlasting punishment. What but love could move him to have mercy upon such a world?

Consider the Saviour provided — not an angel, not the most exalted of his creatures, but his Son, his only begotten Son. What but love could move him to appoint such a Saviour?

Consider the manner in which he was sent — as a gift, a free, unmerited gift: 'God ... gave his only begotten Son.' What but infinite love could give such an unspeakable gift?

Consider the blessings conferred through this Saviour — deliverance from hell and the enjoyment of everlasting life. What but the love of God could confer such blessings?

Consider the condition upon which these blessings are offered — faith, that humble, self-negating grace, so suitable to the circumstances of a poor sinner, that brings nothing but receives all. What but divine love could appoint so gracious a method of salvation? 'It is of faith, that it might be by grace' (Rom. 4:16).

Consider the indefinite extent, or the universal nature, of the offer, which includes sinners of the very worst character, and makes exception of none: 'Whosoever believeth ... [shall] not perish...' Oh what love this is! But I must leave it as the theme of your meditations, not just during your earthly pilgrimage, but through all eternity. Eternity will not be long enough to pry into this mystery, and it will occupy the understanding of men and of angels down through the revolving ages of eternity.

A challenge to the reader

And now, dear reader, to draw towards a conclusion, I would challenge you about this matter of reconciliation to God through Jesus Christ. I have in this booklet set life and death before you. I have explained to you the method of salvation through Jesus Christ — the only method by which you can be saved, the only method that could afford a gleam of hope to such a sinner as me in my recent approach to the eternal world. And now I would bring the matter home to you, and propose that you consent to be saved in this way, or, in other words, to believe in the only begotten Son of God. I make this proposal to you with all solemnity, and let heaven and earth and your own conscience bear witness that it is made to you.

I also insist on a determinate answer here and now: the matter will not admit of a delay and your duty is so plain that there is no need for time to deliberate. A Roman ambassador, treating about peace with the ambassador of a neighbouring state, if I remember rightly, and finding him wanting to gain time by shuffling and tedious negotiations,

A declaration of love

drew a circle around him and said, 'I demand an answer before you go out of this circle.' Such a circle let the spot where you are reading this message be to you: before you stir from your seat, or put down this booklet, I insist on a full, decisive answer to this question, whether you will, here and now, believe in Jesus Christ, or not?

A possible objection answered

But before I proceed any further, I would remove one stumbling-block out of your way. Someone may object, 'You teach us that faith is the gift of God, and that we cannot believe by our own efforts. Why then do you exhort us to do so? Or how can we be concerned to attempt that which it is impossible for us to do?'

In answer to this I grant that the premises are true, and God forbid I should so much as imply that faith can be produced spontaneously by corrupt human nature, or that you can come to Christ without the Father's drawing you. But the conclusions you draw from these premises are very erroneous. I exhort and persuade you to believe in Jesus Christ because it is when such means are used with sinners, and by the use of them, that it pleases God to enable them to comply, or to work faith in them. I would, therefore, use those means which God is pleased to bless to this end.

I exhort you to believe in order to urge you to make the experiment, for it is making the attempt, and that only, which can fully convince you of your own inability to believe, and till you are convinced of this you can never expect strength from God.

I exhort you to believe because, sinful and enfeebled as you are, you are capable of using various means preparatory to faith. You may engage in prayer, hearing the Word and all the outward means of grace with natural seriousness. You may endeavour to get acquainted with your own helpless condition and, as it were, put yourself in the way of divine mercy. And though all these means cannot *by themselves* produce faith in you, yet it is only in the use of them that you are to expect divine grace to work faith in you. Never yet was it produced in one soul, while that person was lying supine, lazy and inactive.

An urgent appeal

I hope you now see good reasons why I should exhort you to believe, and also perceive my design in it. I therefore renew the proposal to you that you should, here and now, as a guilty, unworthy, self-despairing sinner, accept the only begotten Son of God as your Saviour and fall in with the gospel method of salvation, and I once more demand your answer. I would by no means, if possible, take my leave of you till I have successfully called on you to exercise faith in Jesus, my blessed Lord and Master. I am strongly bound by the vows and resolutions of a sickbed to set him before you as the Saviour you need; and now I would endeavour to perform my vows. I would have each one of us give our consent to God's covenant, that we may go on our way through life justified before him.

I persuade and exhort you so to do, in the name and by the authority of the great God; by the death of Jesus Christ for sinners; by your own most urgent and desperate need of him; by all the glorious blessings proposed in the gospel and by the dreadful curse pronounced against unbelievers.

A declaration of love

The blessings that follow from believing

All the blessings of the gospel — pardon of sin, sanctifying grace, eternal life and whatever else you may want — will become yours here and now, if you will only believe in the Son of God. Then let desolation overrun the land; let public and private calamities crowd upon you and make you as poor and afflicted as was Job — still your main interest will be secure; the storms and waves of trouble can only bear you to heaven and hasten your passage to the harbour of eternal rest. Let devils accuse you before God; let conscience indict you and condemn you as guilty; let the fiery law make its demands upon you — you have a righteousness in Jesus Christ that is sufficient to answer all demands and, having received it by faith, you may plead it as your own in law. Happy are all those of whom this is true! Rejoice in hope of the glory of God, for your hope will never make you ashamed!

A warning to those who refuse to believe in Christ

But I expect that some of my readers will refuse to comply with this proposal. This, alas! has been the usual fate of the blessed gospel in all ages and in all countries; as some have received it, so some have rejected it. The old complaint of Isaiah has been justly repeated thousands of times: 'Who hath believed our report? And to whom is the arm of the Lord revealed?' (Isa. 53:1). And is there no reason to pour it out from a broken heart over some of you, my dear readers? Are you all this day determined to believe? If so, I pronounce you blessed in the name of the Lord, but if not, I must pronounce your doom.

I solemnly warn you, on behalf of the living God, that if you continue thus in unbelief, you shut the door of mercy against yourselves and exclude yourselves from eternal life. Whatever splendid appearances of virtue, whatever amiable qualities, whatever seeming good works you may have, the express sentence of the gospel lies in full force against you: 'He that believeth not shall be damned' (Mark 16:16). 'He that believeth not is condemned already, because he hath not believed in the name of the only begotten Son of God' (John 3:18). 'He that believeth not the Son shall not see life; but the wrath of God abideth upon him' (John 3:36). This is your doom repeatedly pronounced by the one whom you must own to be the best Friend of human nature, and if he condemns, who can justify you?

I also warn you that you will not only perish, but that you will perish in a particularly dreadful manner. You will fall with no common ruin. You will envy the lot of heathens who perished without the law, for you incur the particularly heinous guilt of rejecting the gospel and treating the Son of God with contempt. This is an especially daring form of wickedness and the sin that God resents above all the other crimes of which human nature is capable. This is the reason why it is said that Christ came for judgement as well as for mercy into this world and is set for the fall as well as the rising again of many in Israel (Luke 2:34). You now enjoy the light of the gospel, which has conducted many through this dark world to eternal day, but remember also that 'This is the condemnation [that is, it is the occasion of the most heightened condemnation], that light is come into the world, and men loved darkness rather than light' (John 3:19). On this principle Jesus pronounced the doom of Chorazin and Bethsaida to be more intolerable than that of Sodom and

Gomorrah (Matt. 11:21-22). And might it not be hard to find a place where the doom of unbelievers is likely to be so terrible as among those to whom the gospel has been set forth in such a way as I have done here?

And now does not all this move you? Are you not alarmed at the thought of perishing — of perishing by the hand of a Saviour whom you have rejected and despised; perishing under the stain of his blood which you have profaned; perishing not only under the curse of the law, but under that of the gospel, which is vastly heavier? Oh! Are you hardy enough to risk incurring such a doom? This doom is unavoidable if you refuse to comply with the proposal now made to you.

I must now conclude my attempts to reason with you, but to clear my own name, I must call on witnesses to confirm that I have endeavoured to discharge my commission, whatever reception you give it. I call heaven and earth and your own conscience to witness that life and salvation have been offered to you in this booklet through Jesus Christ, and if you reject this offer remember it, that you may bear witness for me at the supreme tribunal, that I am clear of your blood. Alas! You will remember it among a thousand painful reflections millions of ages hence, when the remembrance of it will rend your heart like a vulture. Many gospel messages forgotten on earth are remembered in hell and haunt the guilty mind for ever. Oh that you would believe, and so prevent this dreadful effect from the reading of this booklet!

1. The sermon on which this booklet is based was preached in October 1757, shortly after Davies' recovery from a severe bout of illness.